Chris

To my friend and
mentor

Lefty

Today's Hidden Racism:

A Polite Apartheid

Dave Lefkowith & A.J. Nino Amato

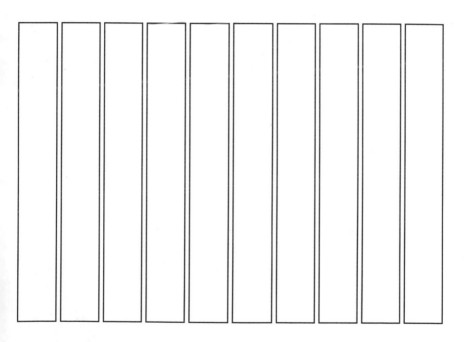

Published by:
The Foundation to End Polite Apartheid
P.O. Box 25400
Los Angeles, CA 90025
www.politeApartheid.com

Library of Congress Control Number: 2001092634
ISBN 0-9712489-0-7

Printed in the United States of America

"One of the greatest challenges our nation continues to face is racism. This book highlights that it is important for every American – including political leaders, business executives, community activists, parents and children – to meet this challenge and to do our part to ensure that we are truly one nation with liberty and justice for all."

U.S. Senator Russell D. Feingold
(Wisconsin)

"Nino and David put forth a simple plan for a specific audience in this book. What is proposed is a solid beginning to build bridges with key leaders in our society and to begin the process of nurturing allies who will work to dismantle the hidden racism that pervades our society."

Lucía Nuñez
Executive Director, Centro Hispano of Dane County

"In many ways, today's racism is far more dangerous than the overt racist hate groups. It is accepted and institutionalized and continues to *kill* the spirit, will and self-worth of every generation of people of color. This book is important because it recognizes the role that white people can and must play to fight our country's new form of racism."

Joyce Bembry
business executive

"To execute the guiding principles prescribed in this gem of a book would positively transform racial conditions on all levels, thereby embracing the oneness of human kind."

Professor Richard Davis
University of Wisconsin - Madison
Madison Wisconsin Institutes for the Healing of Racism

"Race relations is an extremely difficult topic to talk about – we realize that there are indeed many issues to overcome, but we rarely know what to do to find a solution. The guiding principles outlined in this book will, if we are willing, take us to a different level of understanding and, hopefully, will make everyone responsible for eradicating racism that we cannot deny exists among us, all of us.

Alfonso Zepeda-Capistran
President
Latinos United for Change and Advancement, Inc. (LUChA)

This book was inspired by the Sullivan Principles, and catalyzed by the following comment by Dr. Julian Bond:

"I want to spend a few moments talking about race. This is not an easy subject for America. How do we talk about race without making some people feel uncomfortable or making them feel as if they're being blamed for something they are sure they did not do? Nonetheless, this is where we must begin."

Dr. Julian Bond
Madison NAACP Freedom Fund Banquet
October 6, 2000

Highlights from *Today's Hidden Racism: A Polite Apartheid*

"You knew where you stood in Mississippi. You thought you were accepted in Madison, Wisconsin but you aren't. There is a polite Apartheid . . ."

Diversity focus group participant
Madison, WI, September, 2000

"Our fundamental contention is that individual action, not just government policy, must drive the fight against today's hidden racism."

"A hidden racism – our polite Apartheid – is particularly difficult to combat. People of color are often excluded from the chambers of influence where initiatives that might address this issue are conceived and deliberated."

Prologue
September 11, 2001 Impact

We were full of enthusiasm as we completed the editing of this book and got ready for publication during the fall of 2001.

Then September 11, 2001 happened and everything changed.

Immediately, like all Americans, we tried to understand the horror of the terrorist attacks and we rallied around the flag.

On a more mundane level, we were both out of town on September 11 (Nino in Italy, David in Indianapolis), and it took both of us seven days to get home.

But we got home, we took inventory – thank God our families and friends were safe – and we tried to figure out what should come next.

After a great deal of reflection, we've decided to push forward with this book, with The Foundation to End Polite Apartheid, and with our mission to help create a grassroots effort – especially among corporations – to pursue social justice initiatives and fight our country's polite Apartheid.

In the atmosphere of crisis and uncertainty that pervades our country, there is the temptation to put social issues aside. "How can a book on racism matter," some might ask, "in an environment where our country is at war, an unprecedented war with incalculable risks?"

Upon reflection, there are two important reasons to move forward, and we embrace them both.

First, the forces that combine to create a hidden racism in our country continue despite the war on terrorism, and in some cases become more oppressive given the corresponding economic downturn. The impact of racism and social injustice is even more dispiriting when economic conditions are tough. Unequal health care outcomes and job opportunities are more pronounced.

The need to stay focused and active becomes, in some ways, even more important in these times of crisis.

Second, we all agree that times of war require patriotism and a defense of our homeland. But this war is different, and we have to be very careful not to provide the terrorists attacking our country the victory they crave by perverting our free society.

The memory of Japanese (and less well known Italian) internment during World War II no longer seems so remote and unthinkable in an environment when individuals who are Muslims or look like Muslims are attacked and persecuted.

The fact that President Bush — in what may go down as his finest hour — takes care to communicate how individuals can be Arabs and/or Muslims and still be great Americans shows how important it is to attack prejudices and unwarranted assumptions no matter where they occur.

For these reasons — and because we believe in fighting hidden racism wherever it occurs, whatever its genesis — we've decided to push forward, publish this book, activate the Foundation to End Polite Apartheid website, and launch our effort to create a grassroots activism to fight our polite Apartheid.

Let's go!

Today's Hidden Racism: A Polite Apartheid

Table of Contents

Prologue: September 11, 2001 Impact   p 1

Executive Summary   p 4

Dedication   p 6

Chapter 1: What is A Polite Apartheid?   p 10

Chapter 2: Forces that Enable a Polite Apartheid   p 16

Chapter 3: Grassroots Steps to Fight a Polite Apartheid   p 19

Chapter 4: Principle #1: Corporations Need to Get Involved   p 23

Chapter 5: Principle #2: Health Care Imperatives   p 35

Chapter 6: Principle #3: Racial Profiling *Must* End   p 38

Chapter 7: Principle #4: The Role of Faith   p 42

Chapter 8: Principle #5: The Steps Parents Can Take   p 44

Chapter 9: Principle #6: Children Need to "Get Involved"   p 47

Chapter 10: Next Steps: Corporations Must Lead the Way   p 49

Chapter 11: We're Asking for Corporate Leadership   p 55

Appendix: Foundation to End Polite Apartheid Charter   p 57

Executive Summary

The United States is plagued by a pervasive, subtle, persistent racism, far different from the virulent racism that reached a climax in the 1960s, but far more difficult to fight and overcome.

Our fundamental contention is that individual action, not just government policy, must drive the fight against today's hidden racism.

Therefore, we developed six principles (inspired by the Sullivan Principles) to create practical, grassroots initiatives that can address our country's "polite Apartheid."

Six Principles to Combat America's Polite Apartheid

Principle #1:	*Corporations need to get involved in pursuing social justice and equal opportunity, literally from the Board level down*
Principle #2:	*Health care and pharmaceutical corporations need to facilitate mobile family health care programs targeting at risk communities*
Principle #3:	*Local law enforcement agencies must end the practice of racial profiling*
Principle #4:	*Faith communities need to work together to tear down racial and socio-economic barriers*
Principle #5:	*Parents need to take specific, tangible steps to transmit social justice values to their children*
Principle #6:	*Children need to "get involved" through cooperative activities with less privileged communities*

Chapter 10 provides the specific implementation steps we intend to propose to the Fortune 1000 corporations (as well as enlightened companies of any size):

1)   create a customized program to pursue social justice that is easy to implement and enhances shareholder value;

2)   implement a series of performance measures and tracking systems that provide objective confirmation of the corporation's performance in its customized social justice program; and

3)   launch an enthusiastic communications campaign to publicize the corporation's alignment with the six principles to overcome a polite Apartheid, building momentum for suppliers, strategic allies and customers to adopt their own customized social justice programs.

Today's Hidden Racism: A Polite Apartheid

Dedication

Why Did Two Middle-Aged White Guys Write this Book?

Inevitably we realize that people who read this book – probably even those who only hear about it – may well ask:

> "Who *are* these guys? How do two middle-aged white guys have the credentials – where do they get *the right* – to write this book?"

Fair enough.

We recognize that no white person in the United States can ever fully experience the reality of being a person of color for even one day.

But no matter what our color may be, we're not blind to the disturbing forms of racism that are still prevalent in our country, yet seldom discussed by people like us.

In part, our backgrounds as ethnic minorities led us to write this book. We're Jewish and Italian – not racially oppressed in the United States today, but certainly from ethnic backgrounds that kept us separate and apart from the mainstreams where we grew up.

Dave grew up in a segregated community – in New Jersey, in the 1960s and 70s! Dave was a sports nut who never played golf, because the local golf club didn't allow Jews (or blacks or Asians or pretty much anyone who wasn't white and a Republican) to play on the course. Part of growing up Jewish, Italian or Armenian in that community was the realization that you were one of "the dark ones," the people farthest from the mainstream.

Now Dave has a biracial child who has just started to endure the slights that will inevitably increase in frequency and intensity as she grows up – she is unfailingly courageous in her own youthful disdain for racial prejudice, and it's hard not to feel inspired to act by her example.

Nino has a long track record on social justice issues and is a respected business and community leader. Nino grew up in a truly diverse neighborhood in Madison, Wisconsin – where he and his neighborhood friends were brutally taunted by rival high schoolers for their ethnicity. This upbringing – and Nino's loss of a mayoral election as a very young man due to poisonous rumors that his family was part of organized crime – hardened his resolve to seek social justice.

Nino's efforts haven't been unrecognized – he's been honored with both the YWCA Racial Justice Award and the Madison Equal Opportunity Commission's James. C. Wright Humanitarian Award. He is also an active member of the Madison chapters of the NAACP and the Urban League.

So our credentials, such as they are, seem in order. But while we may have good hearts, why is it that we think we can write knowledgeably about racism?

The answer is simple: because people just like us are the ones who must take up the struggle now. A hidden racism – our polite Apartheid – is particularly difficult to combat. People of color are often excluded from the chambers of influence where initiatives that might address this issue are conceived and deliberated.

But we have access to these corridors of power, political and commercial. For over 20 years Dave has consulted extensively with corporations, interacting directly with top management figures. Nino has been a top-level executive within both public and private organizations. We speak their language and we're a comfortable presence.

We have an entrée to advocate for change without being threatening, without being ignored.

Perhaps most importantly – whether we like it or not – *we're part of the privileged elite.* The phenomenon of "white privilege" is totally real, in fact pervasive within large corporations. We can say things and "be heard," while a person of color might be accused of "grinding an ax" or "being defensive."

We feel strongly that we have the affirmative moral obligation to speak up. If people like us *don't* speak up, then there is no way we can get corporate decision-makers to recognize the nearly invisible barriers that keep us apart as a country and threaten our common future.

Our specific purpose in writing this book is to serve as a catalyst, to help awaken and equip a new generation of activists dedicated to positive social change. We're targeting *real change now*, so we intend to be tactical – we intend to advocate for changes that are realistic, that are apolitical, outlining steps that individuals and institutions can take *now* for positive impact **now**.

This is not about good intentions – this about confronting injustice in increments small enough so that local solutions can deliver immediate, local improvements.

We realize that racism won't disappear based on what we write, or on the basis of what anyone writes or does.

But we do have an important mission: ***our vision is to get complacent people with good hearts to see the hidden barriers that create a polite Apartheid, and inspire them to action.***

With the help of every good person our message touches, we hope to overcome these barriers and address our country's silent racism one individual, one company and one community at a time.

We dedicate this effort to our parents, who raised us with the clear notion that the true value of a person lies within.

We dedicate this effort to our children, to whom we want to leave a better world.

Dave Lefkowith
November, 2001

A.J. Nino Amato
November, 2001

Chapter 1
What is A Polite Apartheid?

A Polite Apartheid is the denial to people of color of an equal opportunity to educate their children, keep them healthy and advance their families economically – oppression in the United States by a declining white majority that, in many cases, doesn't even realize how its actions are exclusionary or worse.

We're not talking about the obvious racists with their intolerant religious creeds, hateful websites and violence. These are truly dangerous people and we all recognize them as such. When HBO airs its *Hate.com* specials we're all aghast at the beliefs and actions of these terrorists. Our instinctive reaction is the same one we experienced a generation ago – but with far less urgency, since these racists are clearly recognized to be a marginalized fringe minority with no serious political power or societal influence.

In fact it would be so much easier if this *were* the face of racism in the 21st Century, because this type of hate galvanizes good people to action, just as it did in the 1960s.

Instead, we're talking about a silent epidemic of covert racism. The type of racism that declares segregation to be a thing of the past, even as inner city schools are almost entirely attended by children of color. The type of racism that leads health care providers and pharmaceutical companies to believe they are serving their communities well, when children of color have health statistics that are distressingly inferior to those of white children.

The type of racism that accepts pervasive, persistent inequities in social and economic opportunities and outcomes among different races.

What Racism Was

The authors are two white men in or past their mid-40s. Ours was the generation that was going to end racism.

As children of the 1960s we saw the outrageous racism of Selma, Alabama and Johannesburg, South Africa on our television screens almost every night.

The images of racism that this new medium spilled into our homes and into our consciousness were stark and left a lasting impact: Bull Connors, attack dogs and fire hoses. We witnessed incredibly brave young people, mostly black but some white, fighting for basic rights that we took for granted. We heard the oratory of Dr. Martin Luther King, Jr. that stirred us to action.

And we cried over the horrific image of Dr. King bleeding to death after being shot in Memphis, the specific event that stirred both of us to political consciousness at an early age.

We studied in our schools the historic instances in which Americans practiced overt racism. The horrors of slavery. The inhumanity of exclusionary laws that denied Chinese and Chinese Americans their basic rights. The prejudices that restricted Southern European immigrants from realizing their economic and educational potential. The imprisonment of Japanese-Americans in internment camps during World War II, while their sons fought and bled with immense valor. The genocide of Native Indians. The degradation of migrant workers denied safe working conditions and a fair wage.

Because of television in our homes, ours was the first generation to witness vivid images of brutal repression and racism on a daily basis – the Freedom Riders, Watts, Cesar Chavez, Vietnam. Television did this, television made ignoring injustice impossible. Across a broad spectrum of race and privilege, we knew that what we were witnessing was wrong. We were spurred to action.

Ours was going to be the generation that would defeat racism.

Almost forty years later we've had some successes. Jim Crow died in Selma – Selma now has an African American mayor, for the first time in a city that is overwhelmingly black. Los Angeles narrowly missed electing its first Latino mayor in over a century, but did elect a Latino City Attorney. Asian-Americans, Jews and Italians function pretty much in the mainstream. Working conditions for all peoples have improved.

In fact, we're now becoming sensitive to subtle forms of racism – environmental racism, racial profiling, etc. – that hadn't even been defined during our childhood.

Apartheid died in South Africa, and despite what we all knew to be the continuing struggles by people of color, racism in America seemed to be dying as well.

With the most overt forms of racism apparently defeated, the images on our television changed to other issues both profound and trivial. For a time, we believed that racism was on the run and that our generation's job was done.

But human nature is hard to overcome.

How sad it is to wake up in the new millenium only to discover an ugly truth: racism is alive and virulent. "Jim Crow, Sr." may have died, but "Jim Crow, Jr." is alive and well, part of a silent racism, a "polite Apartheid" that is far more difficult to discern and therefore far more dangerous and difficult to combat.

Racism Today

The racism we must recognize and confront today has a far subtler hue. It's a racism that excludes instead of oppresses. It's a racism that is gentle on the surface but unrelenting and horribly damaging at its core. It's a racism that is creating a self-contented over-class in America.

The understanding that a subtle but pervasive racism persists in the United States is acknowledged by dry government reports. For example, the September, 2000 *Initial Report of the United States of America to the United Nations Committee on the Elimination of Racial Discrimination*, co-sponsored by the Justice Department and the State Department, clearly states in its Introduction:

> "[T]he American people can point with pride at the great strides towards equality made over the past half-century. However, despite these enormous accomplishments, much remains to be done to eliminate racial discrimination altogether. While the scourge of officially-sanctioned segregation has been eliminated, de facto segregation and persistent racial discrimination continue to exist. The forms of discriminatory practices have changed and adapted over time, but racial and ethnic discrimination continues to restrict and limit equal opportunity in the United States. For many, the true extent of contemporary racism remains clouded by ignorance as well as differences of perception. ***Recent surveys indicate that, while most Whites do not believe there is much discrimination today in American society, most minorities see the opposite in their life experiences.***"
>
> *[emphasis added]*

Unfortunately, this quiet, polite Apartheid continues today because too many complacent, increasingly affluent white people allow this to be so. Times are generally good, and we don't have those poisonous images of Bull Connors and fire hoses spewing into our homes.

It's only when we come face-to-face with this persistent, subtle racism that one realizes how terribly sad, unjust and infuriating this polite Apartheid is:

⇒ in a Madison, Wisconsin focus group we hear about four custodial employees who suffer chemical burns to their eyes. Three are white, one is black. The three white employees have patches placed on their injured eyes, and then receive rides home from their colleagues or supervisors. The one black employee is treated, but then left to take a bus home – none of this person's white colleagues "felt comfortable" driving into a neighborhood where people of color were the majority;

⇒ in an affluent suburb outside of Milwaukee, homeowners (who are overwhelmingly white) band together to discuss ways to stop the influx of new neighbors who are "from Chicago" – and who just happen to be, as often as not, people of color;

⇒ in San Diego and Chicago, companies fire workers for speaking their native language (in this case Spanish) during breaks, even though their job responsibilities revolve around their language capabilities. Even worse, after one of these companies was successfully sued for discrimination by fired employees, the owners fraudulently declare bankruptcy and transfer their company assets to avoid the legal penalties;

⇒ at an industry conference, pharmaceutical company executives indicate: "There are programs in our country so that everyone who wants our drugs can get them" – a statement totally at odds with the fact that children of color in our inner cities, for a variety of reasons that certainly are not the responsibility of the drug companies, seldom see health care professionals and have limited access to important health-related programs for which they might be eligible.

Because we're not forced to *confront* these uncomfortable truths – they aren't making headlines, they don't lead off the 6pm news or CNN – we've chosen by default to ignore them.

So it turns out that Jim Crow is alive after all. He (or she) lives in mainstream America, may have all the right "politically correct" instincts – but, knowingly or unknowingly, countenances a thriving racism that continues to institutionalize injustice along racial lines and widen the yawning economic and social justice chasms in our society.

Chapter 2
Personal and Societal Forces that
Enable a Polite Apartheid

Jim Crow, Jr. lives – a polite Apartheid abides – because we allow this silent racism to exist by default. We're too busy with our lives and our careers to notice it, let alone do anything about it.

From a personal perspective, the reasons why a polite Apartheid can exist in America are convincingly articulated by Robert Putnam, in his book *Bowling Alone: The Collapse and Revival of American Community*:

> "Television, two-career families, suburban sprawl, generational changes in values – these and other changes in American society . . . threaten educational performance, safe neighborhoods, equitable tax collection, democratic responsiveness, everyday honesty and even our health and happiness."

The two of us are subject to these same forces that make it so easy to be inwardly focused. We cart our kids frantically from activity to activity in our SUVs, leaving very little time for family members to explore their role in the broader community. The most memorable images television pipes into our homes today are not of King or Kennedy – they are the images of New Economy billionaires and busts, or millionaire game show winners and survivors.

Children today are programmed at an early age to dedicate their efforts to one sport, to excel in a chosen activity, to narrow their pursuits rather than broaden their vision. Their parents – many of them divorced with blended families or single heads of households, all of whom are chronically short of time and sleep – suffer from the same tunnel vision, with focus on job and family blotting out the energy to notice anything else.

We know from personal experience that it's hard to worry about racism you can't see – that you might not even believe exists, and that you *certainly* don't contribute to – when you're consumed by the urgent needs of your family and your job hammering at you every hour of the day.

From a broader societal perspective there are three underlying elements to the polite Apartheid: 1) unequal education; 2) unequal economic opportunity; and 3) growing separation by race. Unfortunately, these three elements reinforce one another.

The unprecedented decade long economic expansion that recently ended papered over this outbreak of polite Apartheid. Almost perversely, overall affluence increased while the degree of disparity in outcomes widened.

For most people, the answer to Ronald Reagan's famous question is clear: even given the post-September 11, 2001 economic downturn, we are generally far better off than we were five or ten years ago. Increasing wealth has enabled those blessed by the new economy to buy new homes, move to more desirable locations and buy more toys.

Affluent white people are moving into new homes in new communities by the score. These communities are beautiful, they are a blessing to the people who live there. They have wonderful schools (public or private) and they represent what seems to be an appropriate outcome for personal success.

But the unintended outcome of this affluence has been a re-segregation of our educational system – white flight to suburban public schools or private education, and (frequently substandard) public education in poorer communities for children of color. The invisible hand of our economy has silently gerrymandered educational opportunity with inevitable and profound social and economic consequences.

What's doubly unfortunate is that an education gap today is more damaging and discriminatory than ever before. The 1990s economic expansion was a "knowledge economy" expansion that dispro-portionately favored the most highly educated segment of our knowledge workforce – an increasingly affluent knowledge workforce far more white than the rest of America.

So these three forces have combined to create a powerful negative momentum, separating America by race, by economic circumstance and by educational opportunity.

The combination of these societal forces and the personal pressures on individuals explain why many white people even question whether or not racism is truly that pervasive in today's society.

In fact, when we talk about this subject in public, we're often accused (silently in written evaluations, *never* in comments made or questions asked out loud during a presentation) of "playing the race card."

But our answer to this is simple: *"If you're a person of color, the race card is played every day."*

And every time we say this in public, every person of color nods his or her head *emphatically*, while the white audience (for the most part) just quietly – politely – listens.

Chapter 3
Grassroots Steps to Fight a Polite Apartheid

First we have to accept that this polite Apartheid exists and abides, threatening now and into the future to rip our country apart into havens of privilege and ghettos of despair.

Second, we have to realize – concede – that the government cannot address this issue unilaterally. The only way for us to overcome the subtle barriers of polite Apartheid is to develop overwhelming grassroots efforts to identify and address this silent epidemic.

This concession bears repetition and amplification.

Government alone can't stop hate. Government alone can't stop racism.

Certainly government must create an atmosphere in which hate is punished, not condoned, in which racism is aggressively prosecuted, not enabled.

But we can't – and shouldn't – expect government bureaucracies to lead the fight against racism in the 21st Century.

We all realize that government agencies are subject to the tyranny of the status quo – they have become terribly unwieldy agents of change. Earlier we quoted from the *Initial Report of the United States of America to the United Nations Committee on the Elimination of Racial Discrimination* co-sponsored by the Justice Department and the State Department. We took the most lucid, most pointed excerpt from a report that ranged over 100 pages – and (in our opinion) this one paragraph conveys the entire power of the full report.

Yet, as government bureaucracies will do, the report belabors its subject for page after mind-numbing page. The bulk of the text is a report on what various government bureaucracies have done to combat racism in the United States.

Which is why this report and its alarming, important observations immediately sank into obscurity.

We don't want to belittle the steps our government is taking, and we don't want them to stop. Specifically, we don't question the motivation of the literally thousands of good people who worked on the initiatives described in this report, nor do we want their motivation to push forward towards social justice to be diminished one iota.

Yet at the end of the day, a polite Apartheid persists in America precisely because another giant report sits on a shelf, people hurry busily on their daily routines – and there is absolutely no urgency for change.

Government bureaucracies alone can't make change. They can enforce important laws and policies which, in the area of racial justice, are usually initiated by some passionate grassroots effort.

As for diversity and affirmative action, we don't want to get pulled down into the morass of debating whether or not these programs work, whether or not new hate crime laws should be on the books and/or how they should be enforced.

These are arguments that occur at a policy level – and ***our fundamental contention is that individual action, not just government policy, must drive the fight against today's hidden racism.***

Therefore, we developed six principles – inspired by the six Sullivan Principles that helped topple Apartheid in South Africa – that offer concrete steps that individuals and corporations can take to address America's persistent racial divide.

These aren't stirring principles that require massive government programs, or charismatic leadership from on high.

Instead, these are common sense steps that everyday people can take to help end our polite Apartheid.

Perhaps most importantly, these principles share three critical characteristics:

1) <u>they are practical</u>. These principles indicate actions that *anyone* and *any organization* can take. Today. No policy deliberations required.

   Are bigger solutions on a broader palette required? You bet. **But our strongly held belief is that immediate local action is more likely to create a critical mass to fight today's polite Apartheid than any broader policy initiatives;**

2) <u>they require one person to initiate, and at most a small team to implement</u>. We don't need a lot of discussion to get this ball rolling. If only a few dozen (or hundred or thousand) people reading this book are motivated to action, then we've accomplished our mission. We intend to create a positive momentum for change at the grassroots level that proves effective, enduring and contagious; and

3) <u>their impact can be measured</u>. We've learned the same thing as parents that we learned as executives: ***"What gets measured gets done."*** Therefore, we've committed ourselves to recommending easy-to-implement local initiatives that individuals and organizations can monitor and measure. Success will build upon success. And failure can be diagnosed, addressed and overcome.

This is our agenda – the reason why we wrote this book, and why these are the principles we'll be pursuing for years to come.

Here are the six principles we recommend to combat America's persistent racial divide:

Six Principles to Combat America's Polite Apartheid

Principle #1:	***Corporations need to get involved in pursuing social justice and equal opportunity, literally from the Board level down***
Principle #2:	***Health care and pharmaceutical corporations need to facilitate mobile family health care programs targeting at risk communities***
Principle #3:	***Local law enforcement agencies <u>must</u> end the practice of racial profiling***
Principle #4:	***Faith communities need to work together to tear down racial and socio-economic barriers***
Principle #5:	***Parents need to take specific, tangible steps to transmit social justice values to their children***
Principle #6:	***Children need to "get involved" through cooperative activities in less privileged communities***

Chapter 4
Principle #1: Corporations Need to Get Involved

Principle #1: Corporations need to get involved in pursuing social justice and equal opportunity, literally from the Board level down

We know so many executives at large organizations whose hearts are in the right place. But their corporations do less than they could to combat racism and promote social justice.

Some executives may tell you that this isn't their mission: they clearly believe their mission is to maximize shareholder value.

We respectfully dispute this – corporations have many more stakeholders than just their shareholders, and these stakeholders have interests beyond short-term return.

But let's avoid that argument to focus on the key issue we believe should be dominant:

> **Most corporations do less than they can to combat economic and racial divides in our country.**

Less than they can and less than they should, when you consider that there are simple steps corporations can take to fight for social justice *and* increase shareholder value beyond expected results at the same time.

One reason corporations do less than they can and should may be because top corporate officers are sheltered from the unpleasant realities that create our polite Apartheid.

In many cases – not always, but often – top executives are sheltered from experiencing even middle class frustrations. For example, they don't know about the frustrations surrounding air travel – especially post-September 11, 2001 – because their travel is usually first class (and increasingly in private jets).

They may not realize how expensive gas or electricity has become because the financial impact on their households is minimal given their six, seven or eight figure incomes.

And if top executives don't have to deal with these ordinary middle class frustrations, then they may not have any way to understand and address the far more desperate issues plaguing so many people of color in our country.

Our intent is not to place blame on these executives for success – they streamline their lives and organize their activities the way they do because their time is valuable.

But the potential contribution of top corporate executives in promoting social justice is invaluable. We need to do a better job of harnessing that potential contribution and making it real.

Therefore, our first suggestion is simply to make sure that top executives of the most powerful corporations in our country have some way to gain a first hand experience of the hidden racism that plagues our society.

We need to strip away the insulation that might prevent the 10,000 most powerful Board members in the United States and our nation's 40,000 top executives from experiencing the full individual, societal and economic cost of our polite Apartheid.

We need to create an awareness, a consciousness – perhaps even an enthusiasm for change – among the most privileged and powerful, because we believe that their human instincts will take over and that they'll respond positively to address the inequities they see.

Therefore, we call upon (at a minimum) the Fortune 1000 companies to commit to a comprehensive program of corporate involvement with at risk communities in their "home towns" and in markets where they sell their goods and services.

We intend to make it simple for corporations to structure their involvement in overcoming our country's polite Apartheid by offering a simple report card in six areas of corporate contribution to social justice.

And we intend to develop an objective, activity-based grading system that every Fortune 1000 company and its external stakeholders can use to determine its success in promoting and pursuing social justice.

As pictured on the following page, our "Corporate Social Justice Report Card" has six possible "Social Justice Subjects," each with objective standards for earning top marks.

Our goal: to help corporations develop their own customized program of social justice initiatives, based on their current efforts, "best practices" from comparable companies, and the various initiatives described in our Corporate Social Justice Report Card:

The Corporate Social Justice Report Card

Social Justice Subject	Objective Grading Criteria to Earn an "A"
1) Commitment to top management presence	Hold one Board meeting per year in an at risk neighborhood, utilizing local services, promoted locally to maximize attendance by (and dialogue with) local residents, followed by a corporate Leadership Council meeting at the same venue
2) Commitment to at risk neighborhoods	Develop and implement a comprehensive "Neighborhood Revitalization Strategic Plan" for a targeted at risk neighborhood, featuring specific, measurable goals and supported by top performing employees in partnership with neighborhood residents
3) Commitment to "social justice sabbaticals"	Institute 60 to 120 day social justice sabbaticals that enable high potential executives to contribute to specific, measurable "hands on" social justice initiatives
4) Commitment to public education	Contribute used (and new) IT equipment to local public schools, along with the technical expertise needed to operationalize the equipment (including instructors)
5) Commitment to job training and internships	Implement a Youth Enrichment internship program within the company *as well as* a scholarship program for technical college training
6) Social Justice goals as an "on /off" switch for executive bonuses	Require that the corporation meet its customized social justice goals (based on the initiatives described in this report card or others) to enable the release of 25% or more of annual executive bonuses

Let's review each of these grading areas, one at a time.

<u>Top Management Presence</u> - the first step corporations can and should take to enhance social justice is simply "showing up."

The easiest and most symbolically powerful way for corporations to "show up" is to hold a full-fledged Board of Directors meeting each year in an at risk inner-city location.

Simply getting these powerful Board members and top executives out into communities where a polite Apartheid is very real and present is a start. But the best performing companies:

- will use local vendors;

- will publicize the Board meeting locally, to hold a Q&A session after normal Board business is transacted to gain the input and perspective of local residents;

- will meet with local community and religious leaders to collaboratively discuss ways in which the corporation can contribute to that specific community's well being;

- will hold concurrent job fairs to promote employment of area residents; and

- will hold, as a follow-up to the Board meeting, a meeting of top corporate executives at the same venue.

The direct economic impact of this policy might be small, but regularly holding important meetings of powerful corporate players in at risk neighborhoods will be symbolically important. These corporations will be signaling with their actions that they possess the courage to expand their corporate agenda and truly embrace equal opportunity.

Just as importantly, corporate executives will gain a first-hand view of what reality is for a growing percentage of the country's population (especially its young population).

We want to make sure that these CEOs and top corporate executives *see* the real conditions that create a polite Apartheid *and then do something about it.*

The second step corporations can and should take to enhance social justice and promote equal opportunity is to illustrate their commitment to an at risk neighborhood in their hometown.

A Neighborhood Revitalization Strategic Plan – in the best case scenario, corporations will launch homegrown, locally-designed "Neighborhood Revitalization" programs to create a sense of ownership and identity within the company for the targeted at risk neighborhood.

For each targeted neighborhood, corporate employees will work collaboratively with area residents, local businesses, and community and religious leaders to develop a specific revitalization plan, citing goals, measurable outcomes, budgets, roles and responsibilities.

These local stakeholders will be the "owners" of this effort, and will promote their plan among local residents. *Corporate executives must curb their urge to be in control.* Then, with a clear path to proceed and with local support and participation, the corporation would assign a rotating support team of employees to staff and help propel this Neighborhood Revitalization program forward.

<u>Social Justice Sabbaticals</u> – to support Neighborhood Revitalization initiatives and a wide variety of other worthwhile initiatives, corporations should allow top performing executives to take periodic "social justice sabbaticals" during their careers.

Pragmatically, locally designed and staffed Neighborhood Revitalization initiatives won't achieve their full intended goal unless corporations assign effective, proven contributors from within their ranks to support local leaders and activists in managing these efforts.

Unfortunately, most busy executives can't or won't make time to volunteer for this type of initiative in addition to their already crushing professional and personal obligations.

But if each Fortune 1000 corporation were to adopt the practice of allowing "high trajectory stars" to choose a rotation assignment in charge of their company's Neighborhood Revitalization program, this initiative would become a major point of corporate pride.

In fact, we believe that this specific recommendation is "pareto optimal," a win-win situation for all involved:

⇒ locally designed Neighborhood Revitalization plans will be far more effective in achieving community-established objectives if the best and the brightest within each corporation are assigned to support these projects;

⇒ corporations will be able to deliver the greatest possible results to their community stakeholders by assigning their top achievers to support these programs;

⇒ the "Social Justice Sabbatical" executives will advance professionally, since their performance in this assignment should be one important way the organization will assess their suitability for senior executive promotions; and

⇒ *most executives will value and appreciate the opportunity to contribute their professional and personal abilities to a community-based initiative.*

That's the beauty behind this recommendation – we're confident that the individuals who become involved will very much *want* to participate in these community initiatives; that's where their hearts are (at least in many cases). During the normal course of their career they'll never find the time – they're just *too busy*.

But a short 60 to 120 day executive sabbatical is not a material sacrifice for a corporation when the benefits to both the corporation and to the executive (in terms of real world experience, exposure, personal fulfillment and community contribution) are so substantial.

Let's be clear: the type of sabbatical we're recommending isn't some temporary assignment with the United Way that concentrates on fund-raising.

We're advocating a hands-on program where something *gets done* – the type of fulfilling initiative where the involved executives will interact directly with local families, businesses and institutions, working hand-in-hand to achieve specific community-based goals.

In the best case scenario, corporate executives will be paired with neighborhood representatives from different cultural and ethnic backgrounds. This team approach may then have two positive outcomes: helping the Neighborhood Revitalization program succeed, while creating a long term personal bond that benefits every person and institution involved.

<u>Commitment to Public Education</u> – the fourth step that corporations can take to contribute to social justice is to support local public education.

Our specific recommendation in this regard is for corporations to contribute all used PCs and relevant new and used IT equipment to inner city schools, and include with this hardware the technical assistance and tutorial help that enables students to use the computers effectively.

This is another "win-win" scenario. Even the oldest, "clunkiest" PC has the potential to immeasurably enrich the life of some student who's currently doing without. But the problem for public school systems is that too many old PCs create a "Tower of Babel" within the school's IT infrastructure.

So, in addition to contributing used (and perhaps some new) PCs, corporations should ensure that they include the minimum software necessary for kids to use the computers effectively, as well as enough volunteer expertise to help teach the kids how to use computers.

In the best case scenario – perhaps working through local Chambers of Commerce or in cooperation with a social justice organization such as the NAACP or the Urban League – donated PCs would come with a standard usage/skill development curriculum and standard testing mechanisms, to build a common set of skills among less advantaged public school students.

Besides just contributing hardware, the truly committed corporations will encourage employees to provide the type of person-to-person tutoring that will help close the academic achievement gap between white children and children of color.

In Madison, Wisconsin, for example, the "School of Hope" initiative (a public/private partnership) enlisted more than 500 citizen-volunteers to tutor elementary school students to improve their academic scores. Many participating corporations allowed employees to take time off for this tutoring assignment as long as they wanted to stay involved.

And now – after five dedicated years – academic achievement test scores for students of color are starting to show noticeable improvement.

Job Training and Internships – the fifth area of contribution by corporations is one that has more than a bit of self-interest involved: support by corporations for job training and internship programs among minority high school (and college) students.

Demographic trends are powerful – and current demographic trends indicate an increasingly large percentage of minority young people should be entering the workforce at a time when workforce shortages are endemic.

Further, perhaps our country's most important and under-utilized educational resources – community and technical colleges (for information technology workers, nurses, electricians, and other trades) – are desperately seeking new students to fill the growing employment demands of corporations and public institutions.

Therefore, the most enlightened and self-interested corporations will develop scholarship programs at community and technical colleges that include tuition grants, internships and most importantly new job opportunities for *all* young job applicants.

This is another situation where everyone wins. The corporation will invest thousands in "Youth Enrichment Scholarships." Students entering the workforce will learn new skills, and find new opportunities for personal and professional fulfillment. And the company will ultimately receive millions of dollars in value, in terms of a highly capable, highly dedicated, highly loyal future workforce.

<u>Tying Executive Bonuses to Corporate Social Justice Goals</u> – finally, we believe that the recommendation that ties all of these initiatives together is linking executive compensation to success in achieving social justice goals (such as the five initiatives described above).

This type of linkage – between social justice and compensation – also addresses a lingering, troubling aspect of the corporate world: the dreaded "glass ceilings."

Anyone who doesn't realize that there are still glass ceilings within major corporations limiting women and people of color from appropriate advancement and compensation is in denial.

The *New York Times* captured this perfectly on the front page of their business section when they pictured the top management team at one of the world's most admired companies (which was, with very few exceptions, entirely male and pale).

We don't intend to argue the merits of executive diversity. Whether they're convinced on the merits – or because they just don't want to buck what's politically correct – all Fortune 1000 companies accept that they must make a commitment to diversity.

And if all Fortune 1000 companies required top management to achieve significant, measurable social justice goals – such as executive diversity goals, or social justice sabbaticals goals, or *whatever* – as the "on/off" switch for at least 25% of its annual bonus, corporations would achieve these goals.

Once again, ***"What gets measured gets done – <u>and what gets rewarded gets pursued!</u>"*** If all Fortune 1000 companies develop customized social justice goals and tell their top executives: "Achieve these goals if you want to earn your full bonus," then the momentum within corporate America in support of pursuing important social justice initiatives would be profound and lasting.

Importantly, this social justice "on/off" switch shouldn't be a threat to management, because corporations are free to develop the social justice goals best suited to their current situation, organizational capabilities and strategic goals.

In fact, it should be easy to gain perfect alignment between the social justice goals of an organization and its overriding shareholder value goals.

We urge Fortune 1000 corporations to publish their own internally-developed social justice goals, which could range broadly both in terms of timeframe (annual to multi-annual) and focus (internship programs, executive demographic census, vendor participation, social justice sabbaticals, neighborhood revitalization programs, etc.).

We will then track the success of these firms in meeting and exceeding their self-instituted goals – *while publicizing how major corporations are multiplying their social justice contributions in the communities they serve.*

Chapter 5
Principle #2: Health Care Imperatives

Principle #2: Health care and pharmaceutical corporations need to facilitate mobile family health care programs targeting at risk communities

After the broad scale of our first principle, this second principle might seem a bit smaller, more focused.

But the disparity in health care access and outcomes among white children and children of color is simply too glaring and dispiriting to countenance.

Our second principle to promote social justice is for relevant corporations (health care providers, HMOs, pharmaceutical companies, medical device manufacturers, appropriate packaged goods companies, etc.) to implement mobile family health care programs.

From a clinical perspective, this may not be the best of all possible worlds. It's hard to keep accurate health care records on people who are being provided medical services out of a mobile van. It's better for patients to develop long-term relationships with caregivers in the traditional health care system, for all the obvious reasons.

But today's health care environment isn't the best of all possible worlds, and for a variety of reasons (good and bad, cultural and economic, lamentable but powerful) children of color just don't receive the same health care – prenatal through to adulthood – that white children receive.

While mobile health vans may not seem like the most effective alternative, they provide increased access by bringing the service to the community rather than requiring the community to come to the service. And current technology developments make it possible to develop centralized, web-based medical record-keeping systems that could overcome many of the current objections to this service model.

The good news here is that there are corporations already pursuing this course of action.

For example, Procter & Gamble's "Avanzando con tu Familia" program circulates vans in Los Angeles that offer local families basic dental and general health screening and services. This program (co-sponsored by the Latino Medical Association) helps families discover and address core health needs, informs them of industry, government and insurance programs for which they qualify, and provides *and explains* critical health information (e.g. prenatal care, infant care, etc.).

In the big picture, the costs to P&G are minimal. For the people it touches, this service means everything.

Corporations can design specific programs focused on dental care (i.e. regular check-ups, sealants, screenings) and general health care screening, to maximize the benefit of the interaction while also maximizing the opportunity to place these patients/children in the mainstream health care system.

And once designed, these "best practices" mobile health care programs can easily be emulated by other corporations that recognize the need to underwrite and participate in this type of effort.

When this happens, the corporations that *do* make this effort and commitment will be broadly recognized as socially responsible community leaders that care about people. In the long run, these corporations will enhance their brand equity among community minded consumers.

We simply need the right companies to step forward and help us realize this vision.

There is probably no investment that a major corporation could make that would have a more profound, more immediate positive impact on deserving families.

Chapter 6
Principle #3: Racial Profiling *Must* End

Principle #3: Local law enforcement agencies __must__ end the practice of racial profiling

In all of our work in the area of social justice, no practice is more infuriating than racial profiling, specifically DWBB (being pulled over by law enforcement officials for "Driving While Black or Brown").

Even in a post-September 11, 2001 environment, where there is a temptation to implement racial profiling using security as a justification, this practice has a dangerous impact on our social fabric and our democratic way of life.

If we're to be social activists – and if we're to build bridges of commonality and understanding over the racial gaps that divide us – then this is an issue we *must* immediately address.

Once again, there are positive examples that point to the possibility of success. In Madison, Wisconsin, a citizen-driven community task force on race relations convinced local law enforcement officials and the City Council to adopt written and enforceable policies prohibiting racial profiling. In the experience of many in Madison, these policies have led to a greater civility between citizens and peace officers during traffic stops, as well as a heightened public awareness about the issue of racial profiling.

A continued focus on this issue – including education and training, data collection from daily police reports and heightened management oversight by elected officials – has led to real progress in the City of Madison.

Other cities can pursue these initiatives, by implementing citizen-driven policies and by leveraging existing technologies (most notably video cameras on each police cruiser). Unfortunately, there is often resistance on the part of many law enforcement figures who feel that these practices may infringe on their ability to do their jobs.

But the importance of this issue means that we simply have to "draw a line in the dirt," continuing to fight the good fight until reasonable policies that eliminate racial profiling are adopted universally.

Our goal here is simple – to make every citizen in the United States be equal and *feel* equal in the eyes of law, which most certainly is not the case currently.

Madison's experience suggests that the best way to proceed in addressing racial profiling is to create a Citizen's Task Force, hold public hearings on racial profiling, and engage the community at large by asking citizens of color straightforward questions such as:

- Have you ever experienced racial profiling while driving?

- Where did the event occur?

- Which law enforcement agency was involved?

- What were you doing at the time of the incident?

- What did the officers involved say and do?

- What kind of car were you driving and what was the neighborhood you were stopped in?

- How was the traffic stop handled, how was the incident resolved?

- Give details on how you were treated and how you would expect to be treated differently now and in the future.

The responses to these questions – if properly communicated to both the community and to local officials, including law enforcement personnel – will lead to substantive progress in developing appropriate police policies and preventing future racial profiling by local law enforcement authorities.

We understand that different communities have different relationships with their law enforcement agencies – one of the authors lives in Los Angeles, which right now has a police department struggling to come to terms with the expectations of its community.

We realize that this is not an easy challenge to address.

But there is a growing national momentum to end racial profiling – best articulated by the *End of Racial Profiling Act of 2001*, jointly proposed by Senator Russ Feingold and Representative John Conyers, "support[ed] by members of both political parties, designed to end the offensive practice of racial profiling" – that can help build a local momentum for change.

Leaders like Senator Feingold and Representative Conyers can create the type of enabling laws that help drive beneficial social change on a national basis.

But, once again, our fundamental contention is that individual action, not just government policy, must drive the fight against today's hidden racism.

Committed individuals on a local level need to pay attention to the thousands of details and human interactions that lead to real grassroots change.

Because any movement that seeks to eliminate racial profiling *must* be propelled by strong local activism. Different union contracts, different community standards, different community demographics and different police leadership/management styles will make each situation unique.

We understand that there can be no single approach to helping end the practice of racial profiling.

But we know that there are standard, proven effective tools and approaches that communities can use to examine this issue, understand the dispiriting damage racial profiling causes, and take the first steps to ending this legacy of racism.

We will provide these standard tools and approaches to all communities that request them, helping local activists who step forward to take responsibility for ending racial profiling in their communities.

Chapter 7
Principle #4: The Role of Faith

Principle #4: Faith communities need to work together to tear down racial and socio-economic barriers

Faith plays an important role in American life – while many of us attend formal religious services less often than we used to during our childhood, America is still a God-loving nation.

This was never more apparent than in our nation's response to the unspeakable acts of September 11, 2001 – when our country came together in a melting pot of different races and different religions.

Therefore, it is important to include religious organizations in any attempt to combat racism.

Our recommendation for how faith-based organizations can help fight a polite Apartheid is simple, clear and easy to pursue, because we are appealing to individuals to take a small step: quite simply, *we should all make the effort, at least once a year, to attend a religious service outside our socio-ethno-economic comfort zone.*

Specifically, this means that we should go with our loved ones – at least once a year – to the religious services of another faith. And at least once a year, we should ask those of another faith to join us in our house of worship.

Based on experience, we guarantee that this "religious adventure" will be incredibly uplifting for you and for everyone in the congregation you visit.

We felt so strongly about this recommendation that we discussed this principle with various religious leaders we know and love. The reaction of each was the same: *congregations*, as well as individuals, should be working together, interacting together to bring down the walls that separate us.

In each case, these spiritual leaders immediately discussed with us the times they've pursued exactly this type of initiative, and the ways that they might introduce a "congregation cultural exchange" in the near future.

The best result from following this principle is that your own faith will grow stronger as you begin to understand the faith of others better.

Even more importantly, you will find the people you meet less threatening and less different when you see them before God as God sees them – as God sees us all.

Chapter 8
Principle #5: The Steps Parents Can Take

Principle #5: Parents need to take specific, tangible steps to transmit social justice values to their children

Time pressures of job and family may have eroded the amount of time we contribute to social causes, but America remains a very giving nation. The most recent statistics indicate that Americans gave approximately $200 billion in charitable gifts last year – this is an amazing testament to both our affluence and our inherently generous natures.

Our recommendation is for parents to go one step further – to make giving part of a broader, more meaningful effort to provide their children with an understanding of the issue of social justice.

A first step will provide giving with a larger context – we recommend involving children in an annual family ritual that reviews the charities and community organizations that the family supports, *why* the family supports these causes, and how much the family should give to these causes and others. This ritual should then give each child the opportunity to nominate one charity for support by the family – the child will then have "ownership" of this cause.

This ritual will not only make the child feel good – this approach gives children the opportunity early in their lives to understand key social justice concepts, and to practice *doing something about it* from the very earliest age.

This is the type of "active family approach" to charity that we believe pays the biggest dividends. Instead of making charitable donations via payroll deduction – an automated form of giving that might have a positive net result, but which is absolutely devoid of spiritualism – we hope that parents can talk with their children about the meaning of charity, and the importance of the causes they support.

It doesn't matter what causes one chooses; we're not promoting any specific charitable or political or social agenda here.

But we've found that children are thrilled to be part of such a conversation with their parent or parents – it makes them feel adult, it teaches them about their world and it places before them the realities of others less fortunate.

Participating in the "family giving discussion" makes children feel part of a generous, loving and giving family.

(In fact, perhaps the best time to hold one of these "family giving conferences" is during the year-end holiday season as an antidote to the growing materialism of the holidays.)

Of course, simply "helping those less fortunate" is not enough. Parents need to expose children to different races and cultures in other more personal ways.

Parents can expand their circle of friends to include people of different races and cultures – this type of action "leads by example" in a way that is more powerful than any words a parent could use.

Parents can also encourage their children to play with toys and games from different cultures, and read magazines and books that include stories and characters from different races and cultures.

All of us should be searching for ways to make the culture and habits of "others" more familiar and less threatening to our children.

Through these actions and others, like:

- "social action" days with your religious organization or your children's school,

- family discussions on news topics concerning race and social justice (as a remarkable alternative to television during dinner), and/or

- volunteer activities pursued as a family

we as parents can help overcome our society's silent racial divide, teaching our children the values they will need to make theirs a better world.

Chapter 9
Principle #6: Children Need to "Get Involved"

Principle #6: Children need to "get involved" through cooperative activities in less privileged communities

Finally, we recommend that children develop their own "hands-on" involvement with those who are less fortunate.

If one doesn't already exist, we recommend strongly that children create a "Social Action" club at school. This club should organize initiatives in less advantaged neighborhoods – clean-ups, tutoring, any activity that is age appropriate for the child. This club should also organize activities in which children schedule academic, social and extracurricular activities in *both* schools.

Living in a wealthy, totally white suburb, Dave participated in this type of extra-curricular activity when he was in high school. His daughter participates in this type of activity now. In both generations, this activity breaks through the cocoon of affluence and provides children with a starker, "realer" perspective on how the full spectrum of people in the United States live their lives.

Yes, there is the real threat that these clubs can become a form of *noblesse oblige*, the type of condescending "silk stocking" liberalism that is such a turn-off.

So – recognizing this possibility – we must redouble our efforts to make sure that the exchanges our children participate in are "real," that they add to the common understanding of our diverse society, and that they encourage children to break out of the racial and economic boundaries that separate our society.

Importantly, "culture cuts both ways" – as do ill-founded stereotypes and perceptions. Clearly there is a problem with the white establishment having a hard time understanding the realities of other communities and cultures. But youths in at risk schools are similarly captive of negative stereotypes of an oppressive, racist white establishment.

These interactions among school children, then, are intended to "normalize" race – to eliminate stereotypes and promote an environment of youth empowerment and racial reconciliation.

Our children of affluence need the profound, enlightening experience of breaking through our polite Apartheid. And children in less privileged situations will find out that people of good faith abound on both sides of our country's racial divide.

In the best case scenario, this type of involvement will lead to a renewed streak of social activism in our children's generation, replacing the disturbing anarchistic eco-terrorism that has emerged recently among many young people with a more constructive, uplifting alternative.

We had the "benefit" of galvanizing events like Selma, Vietnam and the first Earth Day to help our generation build an urgent social self-awareness.

For the next generation, let's try to find some context to help our children understand why they should feel an urgent passion to actively support initiatives that seek a more equitable social justice.

Let's harness the very powerful "soccer mom" (and soccer dad) phenomenon – one day a week, one day a month – to educate our children in a way that is fundamentally important for our communities and our country.

Chapter 10
Next Steps: Corporations Must Lead the Way

If the reader has taken care in reviewing our recommendations, it will be apparent that our primary focus is on actions that corporations can take, besides those initiatives concerning local governments, religious organizations, families or individuals.

This emphasis is intentional.

Two forces have combined to make large corporations more powerful and more pervasive than ever before:

1) the unprecedented economic expansion at the end of the 20th Century; and

2) the rapid evolution and application of unprecedented information technologies.

Both of these forces combine to make corporations more effective, more profitable – while at the same time these two forces widen the racial divide in our country.

Therefore, we believe strongly that the evolving notion of corporate accountability must now expand to include a sense of social justice.

The most progressive companies will realize that they "owe" our society some "payback" for their unprecedented prosperity. U.S.-based corporations have benefited enormously from the recent decade of prosperity, and they rightly ought to attribute their success to factors like talent, innovation, courage in the face of uncertainty and hard work. But they also need to acknowledge that American freedom and America's diverse society contribute to their prosperity.

Therefore, these corporations need to recognize that an unprecedented investment in equal opportunity and social justice is necessary to safeguard and continue the long-term returns their shareholders enjoy.

The best, most progressive corporations stepped forward to fight Apartheid in South Africa, to adopt the Sullivan Principles and fight for social justice far from home without being forced to.

We are confident that the same type of progressive, far-sighted corporations will enlist in our quest to adopt the principles outlined in this book, to fight a polite Apartheid at home.

Large corporations can easily implement the specific steps we've recommended with no change in corporate values and no loss of focus on building shareholder value. These changes aren't radical and they won't disrupt an organization – they simply seek to create a continuous, hands-on pressure by corporations to fight racism and enhance social justice.

Further, every corporation of any significant size can afford to – and should – fund the initiatives outlined in this book.

In fact, we believe that taking these steps will dramatically enhance shareholder value through more motivated employees, better stakeholder/community relations, effective institutional marketing and direct return on investment.

So here, at the end of our book, we present the specific challenge we propose to corporate executives at each of the Fortune 1000 companies: the simple three step process we will urge all U.S. corporations to implement in our fight to defeat today's hidden racism.

Three Step Process

There are three steps that every corporation – regardless of its size or industry – can take to fight our polite Apartheid in the United States. Every corporation can:

1) create a customized program to pursue social justice that is easy to implement and enhances shareholder value;

2) implement a series of performance measures and tracking systems that provide objective confirmation of the corporation's performance in its customized social justice program; and

3) launch an enthusiastic communications campaign to publicize the corporation's alignment with the six principles to overcome a polite Apartheid, building momentum for suppliers, strategic allies and customers to adopt their own customized social justice program.

Let's review each of these steps in a bit of detail, and then discuss how every Fortune 1000 company can move forward on a practical, real world basis.

Step 1) Create a customized social justice program – every company is different, so every company should develop its own unique social justice program.

In this book we've outlined a series of initiatives that companies can take to develop a social justice program:

- hold Board meetings (and several related associated functions) in an at risk neighborhood;

- develop and launch one or more collaborative "Neighborhood Revitalization Strategic Plans" – these plans can be customized in terms of steps taken, timeframes and intended goals;

- institute the practice of "social justice sabbaticals," using any reasonable guidelines. We would suggest: a) 60 day minimums; b) based on short proposals by the individual involved; c) targeting specific local actions and results; d) in conjunction with local stakeholders; and e) with specific goals and performance tracking. Each company can develop its own standards and processes for this type of activity;

- launch a program to enhance local public education, including: a) leveraging new and used IT equipment in local schools; and b) providing positive incentives for employees to dedicate their time to tutoring and mentoring students from inner city schools;

- implement Youth Enrichment internship and scholarship programs; and/or

- require the attainment of specific "social justice goals" in order for executives to receive their full targeted bonus amounts.

This broad spectrum of initiatives – *which in some cases will add to the effective programs many corporations are already leveraging to pursue diversity and social justice* – gives every management team plenty of room to find the specific combination of initiatives they can use to build a customized social justice program.

There is no required "minimum" number of initiatives for a corporate social justice program – any two, three, four or more initiatives that a corporation puts together and publicizes will support this fight against our polite Apartheid.

And as more and more corporations take the challenge, a positive momentum will start, a virtuous cycle where companies find that pursuing more and more social justice initiatives creates more and more positive results – thrilled and motivated employees, hugely positive local press coverage, delighted shareholders, supportive local politicians and (perhaps most importantly) empowered communities that have benefited enormously from the corporation's new level of involvement.

Any company can create a customized social justice program that they feel is affordable, consistent with corporate values and implementation-friendly. Every company should.

Step 2) Implement performance measures and tracking systems – remember, "What gets measured gets done." So an integral part of every social justice program *has* to be establishing a series of concrete, objective goals, and then tracking the corporation's performance along these goals.

There is no more culturally standard behavior in corporations than setting goals and achieving goals. This is SOP - standard operating procedure – at major corporations.

But creating and pursuing social justice goals elevates the corporation to a new level of achievement. The motivational benefits – and the bottom line benefits – will be enormous and immediate.

We're not recommending anything elaborate here – companies can adapt easy-to-use goals and tracking systems from "normal" business activities. This will simply be a case of taking something that works in a standard business initiative, and putting these methods to use in a creative new way; and

<u>Step 3) Launch an enthusiastic communications campaign</u> – we believe strongly in "Catching people doing something right."

We encourage corporations that implement social justice programs to launch an enthusiastic communications campaign. *It's their right, they'll deserve the credit!*

Corporations that have the courage and vision to understand why it is necessary and *right* for them to create and launch a social justice program deserve all the positive recognition they can get.

So we recommend strongly that once corporations have designed their customized social justice program, they launch employee information campaigns and institutional marketing initiatives that let the world know: "We understand how our social mission complements our economic mission, and we're pursuing the two in harmony and synergy."

These steps are palpably easy to take.

All we have to do now is get key corporate decision-makers to say: "Yep, I'm in. Let's move forward with our customized social justice program."

We need to encourage the participation of major corporations and their far-sighted leaders. *We simply need to ask for corporate leadership.*

Chapter 11
We're Asking for Corporate Leadership

The next step after writing this book is to get something done.

So, starting immediately, we're going out into the world and *asking for corporate leadership*!

We will send this book to the CEOs of every Fortune 1000 company. We will offer our assistance to help *any* corporation willing to "show leadership" and launch initiatives to overcome our polite Apartheid.

Ultimately, we'd like to see a world where progressive companies *insist* on doing business only with corporations that have a social justice program in place – just as some companies now demand to do business with ISO-qualified firms or firms that are committed to stronger environmental standards, basic living wages and/or advancing cultural diversity within their organization.

To help companies develop their social justice initiatives, we have created a foundation – the Foundation to End Polite Apartheid, or FEPA – with the mission:

> "The Foundation to End Polite Apartheid (FEPA) is a 501(c)(3) public charity that seeks to galvanize corporate leadership, leverage educational activities and inspire individual efforts to overcome today's persistent, hidden racism in the United States.
>
> Our purpose is to serve as a catalyst, providing the expertise and energy necessary to stimulate grassroots efforts to fight racism."

We've included FEPA's charter as an appendix to this book.

A key initiative by this foundation will be the development of a website – www.politeApartheid.org – prominently displaying each corporation's performance versus their social justice goals.

This website will be one way that companies dedicated to implementing social justice programs can get all the positive publicity they deserve.

In addition to these corporate efforts, the Foundation to End Polite Apartheid will send this book to public opinion leaders locally, regionally and nationally. We will ask for their involvement in convincing corporations to take the practical, positive steps we've outlined to fight today's hidden racism.

The Foundation to End Polite Apartheid will also send copies of this book to college activist organizations. We believe the guiding principles in our book provide a positive, actionable message for students: indicating how they can help companies, communities and families take the simple, practical steps necessary to address the persistent, debilitating social inequities that still plague our society.

Most importantly, we will dedicate ourselves to seeking out progressive companies and visionary CEOs who will take the lead in addressing today's hidden racism. We'll focus first on Fortune 1000 corporations, encouraging these and other leading companies to enthusiastically launch social justice programs.

This is an opportunity for everyone involved to make an historic contribution to a transformational positive change in our society.

It is now up to each and every one of us to take some type of action to address today's hidden racism and end our polite Apartheid.

Let's go!

Appendix
Foundation to End Polite Apartheid Charter
(www.politeApartheid.org)

Mission

The Foundation to End Polite Apartheid (FEPA) is a 501(c)(3) public charity that seeks to galvanize corporate leadership, leverage educational activities and inspire individual efforts to overcome today's persistent, hidden racism in the United States.

Our purpose is to serve as a catalyst, providing the expertise and energy necessary to stimulate grassroots efforts to fight racism.

Our immediate goals include:

1) publishing a book that summarizes FEPA's point of view – *Today's Hidden Racism: A Polite Apartheid* – and sending this book to the CEOs of major U.S. companies to enlist their best efforts in fighting racism;

2) helping to develop customized corporate programs that fight racism, building upon the current efforts of "best practices" corporations;

3) publicizing innovative corporate efforts to fight racism, including the development of a website *(www.politeApartheid.org)* that will provide quarterly evaluations of the innovative efforts "best practices" major corporations are making to fight racism;

4) launching a series of speaking engagements to promote the major tenets of our book and corporate campaign, seeking

the support of grassroots activists across the United States; and

5) developing major educational efforts (with topics that support racial reconciliation, youth empowerment and racial harmony) that FEPA will then arrange to provide *pro bono* to local schools.

While these are our immediate goals, we will always retain the flexibility to address emerging opportunities to fight racism.

Perhaps most importantly, we will not engage in policy initiatives or political lobbying – our purpose lies entirely in creating a positive, grassroots momentum to address today's hidden racism, our country's "polite Apartheid."

Foundation Model

FEPA will follow three fundamental tenets in all of its operations:

1) we will provide our support and expertise at cost – we will not seek to create a "financial surplus" when providing services to corporations to fight racism. FEPA will only seek "at cost" reimbursement for our services because our goal is to achieve the broadest possible scope of corporate participation in innovative, grassroots initiatives to fight racism;

2) we will focus on achieving specific, targeted results – we will focus intensely on making sure that our work with key stakeholders achieves tangible, specific results that we can publicize in the press and on our website; and

Reading Level 4.2
Points 1

108754
Alaska

William David Thomas
AR B.L.: 4.2
Points: 1.0   LG

RUSHVILLE ELEMENTARY

ALASKA

by William David Thomas

Gareth Stevens
Publishing

Please visit our web site at: **www.garethstevens.com**
For a free color catalog describing Gareth Stevens Publishing's
list of high-quality books and multimedia programs, call
1-800-542-2595 (USA) or 1-800-387-3178 (Canada).
Gareth Stevens Publishing's fax: (877) 542-2596.

Library of Congress Cataloging-in-Publication Data

Johnston, Lissa.
    Alaska / William David Thomas.
      p. cm. — (Portraits of the states)
    Includes bibliographical references and index.
    ISBN-10: 0-8368-4697-4 ISBN-13: 978-0-8368-4697-3 (lib. bdg.)
    ISBN-10: 0-8368-4714-8 ISBN-13: 978-0-8368-4714-7 (softcover)
    1. Alaska—Juvenile literature. I. Title. II. Series.
    F904.3.T44   2006
    979.8—dc22   2006001899

Updated edition reprinted in 2008. First published in 2006 by
Gareth Stevens Publishing
A Weekly Reader® Company
1 Reader's Digest Rd.
Pleasantville, NY 10570-7000 USA

Copyright © 2007 by Gareth Stevens, Inc.

Editorial direction: Mark J. Sachner
Project manager: Jonatha A. Brown
Editor: Catherine Gardner
Art direction and design: Tammy West
Picture research: Diane Laska-Swanke
Indexer: Walter Kronenberg
Production: Jessica Morris and Robert Kraus

Picture credits: Cover, © Danny Lehman/CORBIS; p. 4, © Tom Bean: p. 5
© Art Today; p. 6 © Hultan Archive/Getty Images; p. 7 © Three Lions/Getty
Images; p. 9 © Bettman/CORBIS; p. 10 © U.S. Navy/Getty Images; p. 12
© Chric Wilkins/AFP/Getty Images; pp. 15,16 © Jeff Greenberg/PhotoEdit;
p. 18 © Pat & Chuck Blackley, pp. 21, 25, 28, 29 AP Images; p. 22
© Susan Van Etten/PhotoEdit; p. 24 © Dave G. Houser/Post Houserstock/
Corbis p. 26 © Gibon Stock Photography; p. 27 © Michael DeYoung/Corbis

Printed in the United States of America

4 5 6 7 8 9 10 09 08

CONTENTS

Chapter 1 Introduction......................4

Chapter 2 History....................6

Time Line...................13

Chapter 3 People.................14

Chapter 4 The Land....................18

Chapter 5 Economy....................22

Chapter 6 Government....................24

Chapter 7 Things to See and Do.............26

Glossary....................30

To Find Out More..................31

Index....................32

Words that are defined in the Glossary appear
in **bold** the first time they are used in the text.

On the Cover: A moving wall of ice meets the ocean in Glacier Bay.
The ice in glaciers is often bright blue.

Introduction

Words like *biggest, tallest,* and *most* are often used to tell about Alaska. It is the largest of the fifty U.S. states. It has higher mountains and more oil than any other state. The list of big things about Alaska goes on and on.

The state has lots of land, but it has few people. Alaska has valleys covered with thick, moving ice. In summer, it has fields covered with flowers. Alaska has modern cities, and it has forests where bears and wolves live. It has few roads but more private airplane pilots than any other state.

Alaskans love their wild, beautiful state. Come for a visit! See what they like about being the biggest, the tallest, and the most.

Alaska's Mount McKinley is the tallest mountain in North America. Its Native Alaskan name is *Denali*. That means "high one."

The state flag of Alaska.

ALASKA FACTS

- Became the 49th U.S. State: January 3, 1959
- Population (2007): 683,478
- Capital: Juneau
- Biggest Cities: Anchorage, Juneau, Fairbanks, Sitka
- Size: 571,951 square miles (1,481,346 square kilometers)
- Nickname: The Last Frontier
- State Motto: North to the Future
- State Flower: Forget-me-not
- State Tree: Sitka spruce
- State Land Animal: Moose
- State Bird: Willow ptarmigan

History

Thirty thousand years ago, some hunters left their homes in Asia. They traveled across a narrow strip of land to reach Alaska. That strip, called a land bridge, is now under water.

The First Alaskans

Among the early settlers in Alaska were the Tlingit people. They lived along the southeast coast. Other people came to Alaska, too. The Haida, from Canada, were known for their beautiful carvings. The Athabascans were some of the first people to use snowshoes.

The Aleut people lived in southwestern Alaska. They built small boats, much like modern **kayaks**. An Aleut word gave the state its name. *Alyeska* means "the Great Land."

Another group of people hunted and fished in the far north. Some people called them Eskimo. They called themselves Inuit.

More than one hundred years ago, these Haida people wore special costumes for a ceremony. They are holding masks and figures carved from wood.

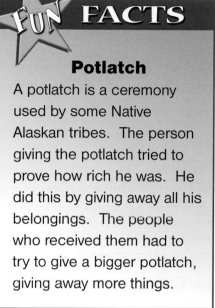

The Russian Fur Trade

In 1741, a Russian sea captain came to Alaska. His name was Vitus Bering. He saw seals and otters with thick fur. Furs were worth a lot of money then. Soon, Russian traders set up camps in Alaska.

The Russians treated the Native Alaskans badly. They killed some of the Native Alaskans. They forced others to find furs for them. Many of the Native Alaskans became sick and died from diseases that the Russians had.

The Russians stayed for more than one hundred years. Traders from other countries came to Alaska, too. Many animals were killed for their fur. Finally, the seals and otters were almost gone.

This is the Russian trading post at Sitka in 1827. From here, ships carried furs to Russia, where the furs were sold for high prices.

Name That Town!

In 1880, a miner in southeast Alaska found lots of gold. Other miners rushed to the spot. His small camp soon became a town. The miner wanted the town to have his name. He gave lots of money to the town's people. They voted to change its name. The miner was Joe Juneau. His old camp is Alaska's capital city, Juneau.

An American Icebox

The United States was interested in Alaska's fish and **minerals**. In 1867, the United States bought Alaska from Russia. It cost just over $7 million. Many Americans thought this was foolish. They called Alaska an "icebox." Others were excited about the new land. They moved to Alaska and went to work. Fishing was the first big business. A fish **cannery** opened in 1878.

Gold!

Miners discovered gold in Alaska in the 1860s. Over the next forty years, more gold was found in this area. Miners also found gold just across the border in Canada. Thousands of people rushed north, hoping to get rich. In Alaska, stores opened to sell

IN ALASKA'S HISTORY

The Soapy Smith Gang

Soapy Smith was a famous Alaskan crook. He came to Skagway during the Gold Rush. He and his gang tricked and cheated miners to get their money. Soon, miners began staying away from Skagway. At last, the town's people had enough. They chased Smith's gang out of town. Soapy was killed in a shoot-out.

goods to the miners. Many hotels and restaurants were built. The **population** grew.

Beginnings of Government

As more people rushed to find gold, Alaskans began to think about their future. They knew they needed more laws and courts. The first code of law was written in 1900. Juneau was named the capital city the same year. The U.S. Congress made Alaska a **territory** in 1912. Soon, people wanted Alaska to be a state.

World War II

In December 1941, the United States went to war with Japan. Japanese soldiers came to Alaska. They landed on

Miners shovel gravel into big pans in the late 1800s. Next, the gravel is washed with water. That separates bits of gold from the sand and stones.

two islands. It was the only time during World War II that foreign soldiers took U.S. land. U.S. soldiers took the islands back from the Japanese in 1943.

Statehood

After the war, the territory of Alaska became very important. Russia and the United States had become enemies. Alaska was very close to Russia. Then, in 1957, oil was found in Alaska. More and more people wanted Alaska to be a state. Alaska became the forty-ninth U.S. state on January 3, 1959.

Oil

Prudhoe Bay is in the far northern part of Alaska. In 1968, workers there drilled holes deep

IN ALASKA'S HISTORY

The Al-Can Highway
When World War II began, there were no good roads going from the United States to Alaska . The U.S. Army began to build one. They worked twenty-four hours a day in snow, wind, and terrible cold. In just eight months, the road was finished. The Alaskan-Canadian Highway was 1,522 miles (2,449 km) long. That was more than sixty years ago. Today, the Al-Can is still the most important road going to Alaska.

These American soldiers are on Attu Island in 1943. They fought to take back the island from the Japanese in World War II.

in the earth. They found the biggest oil field in the United States. Oil brought lots of money to Alaska. Special laws were soon passed. These laws let most Alaskans share some of the oil money.

Oil brought problems, too. In 1989, an oil ship named *Exxon Valdez* ran into some rocks along the coast. The oil from the ship spilled into the ocean. Thousands of birds, otters, and other animals died. It took more than three years to clean up the oil. It cost more than $2 billion.

Today, Alaska is in the middle of a big argument. It is about land and oil. The land is the Arctic National Wildlife Refuge (ANWR). It is home to millions of **caribou** and other animals. There may be a large amount of oil under this land.

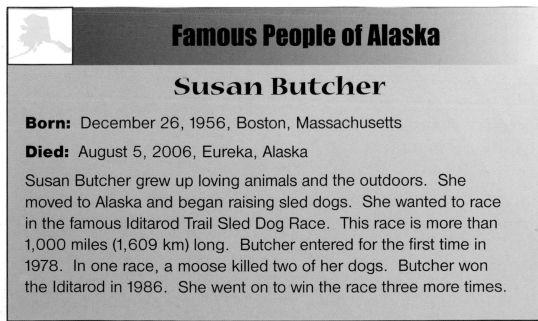

Famous People of Alaska

Susan Butcher

Born: December 26, 1956, Boston, Massachusetts

Died: August 5, 2006, Eureka, Alaska

Susan Butcher grew up loving animals and the outdoors. She moved to Alaska and began raising sled dogs. She wanted to race in the famous Iditarod Trail Sled Dog Race. This race is more than 1,000 miles (1,609 km) long. Butcher entered for the first time in 1978. In one race, a moose killed two of her dogs. Butcher won the Iditarod in 1986. She went on to win the race three more times.

Many clean-up workers helped scrub oil off seaside rocks in 1989. Oil that spilled from the *Exxon Valdez* coated many beach areas.

Some companies want to drill for the oil. Other people want to block the drilling. They think oil wells will hurt the land and animals. The argument is still going on.

IN ALASKA'S HISTORY

Native Alaskan Rights

In 1913, men from many Native groups got together. They formed the Alaskan Native Brotherhood. A group for women, the Alaskan Native Sisterhood, was formed a few years later. They worked to get back land taken by white people. They wanted the right to vote. They also wanted their children to go to good schools. In 1971, the U.S. Congress passed a special law. It was called the Alaska Native Claims Settlement Act. This law gave land and money to Native Alaskans. The law also set up twelve Native **corporations**. They protect the land and manage the money.

★ ★ ★ Time Line ★ ★ ★

Early 1700s	The Haida come to Alaska many, many years after the Tlingit arrived.
1741	Vitus Bering visits Alaska. Russian fur traders soon set up small villages.
1860s	Miners find gold in Alaska and in parts of neighboring Canada. Alaska's population begins to grow.
1867	The United States buys Alaska from Russia.
1912	Alaska becomes a U.S. territory.
1942-1943	Japanese soldiers invade Alaskan islands. They are driven off by the U.S. Army.
1957	Oil is found in Alaska
1959	Alaska becomes the forty-ninth U.S. state.
1964	The strongest earthquake in U.S. history hits Alaska.
1968	The largest oil field in the United States is discovered in Prudhoe Bay.
1971	The Alaska Native Claims Settlement Act gives land and money to Native Alaskans.
1989	An oil tanker spills about 11,000,000 gallons (41,639,530 liters) of oil into the ocean near Alaska.
2006	Talks continue about drilling for oil in the Arctic National Wildlife Refuge.

People

Native Alaskans make up a big group of people in the state. They are the largest non-white group in Alaska. Most of them are Inuit and Aleut. Alaska has a higher percentage of Native citizens than any other state.

People from Many Places

Most Alaskans were not born in the state. They moved to Alaska from other places. Most of them came from other parts of the United States. Others came from

Hispanics

This chart shows the different racial backgrounds of people in Alaska. In the 2000 U.S. Census, 4.1 percent of the people in Alaska called themselves Latino or Hispanic. Most of them or their relatives came from places where Spanish is spoken. Hispanics do not appear on this chart because they may come from any racial background.

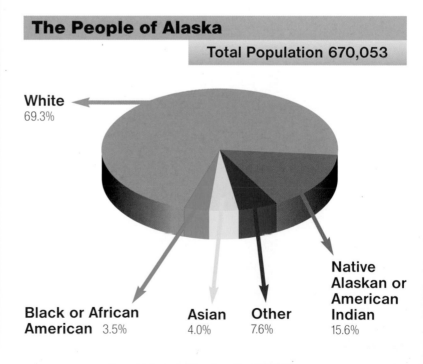

The People of Alaska

Total Population 670,053

White 69.3%

Black or African American 3.5%

Asian 4.0%

Other 7.6%

Native Alaskan or American Indian 15.6%

Percentages are based on the 2000 Census.

Anchorage is Alaska's biggest city. More than 260,000 people live here. It is also the main business center for the state.

Canada and Russia. Smaller numbers of people moved here from Europe and Asia.

People keep coming to Alaska. They come for lots of reasons. Many of them want to find work. The state's oil fields offer lots of jobs. Some people come for the wild, rugged land. Others move here because the state is still young and growing. Alaska is often called "the Last Frontier." People want to be part of it.

Town and Country

Alaska grew very quickly after it became a state. For many years, it grew much faster than the rest of the United States. Today, the population is still growing.

Most Alaskans now live in cities. Anchorage is the biggest city. Over 40 percent of all the people in the state

Alaska's capital city, Juneau, is in the southeastern part of the state. It lies between the Gulf of Alaska and two big mountains. Juneau was once a gold-mining camp. Today, more than 30,000 people live here.

live there. They work in big office buildings. They shop at malls. The children play in parks, and they go to modern schools.

Life is different in **rural** parts of the state. People often live in small villages. These areas have few roads

and, sometimes, no roads at all. People travel by boats or small airplanes. During the winter, they may use dogsleds or snowmobiles.

Religion

Alaska has room for every faith. The first Alaskans had their own religions. Many Native people still follow these old faiths. When the Russians came to Alaska, they built churches. Some of these churches are still there. Today, the state has many kinds of Protestant churches. It has Roman Catholic churches, too. The state also is home to Jews, Buddhists, and people of other religions.

Education

Schools in Alaska's cities are like those in other states. In rural areas, schools may be very small, with only a few students in each grade. The state helps these students with computers. Alaskan students can connect to classes in other schools through the Internet.

The University of Alaska is the biggest university in the state. It has more than twenty-eight thousand students. The largest **campus** is in Anchorage. Other towns around the state have campuses, too. This gives many Alaskans a chance to go to college.

Famous People of Alaska

Elizabeth Peratrovich

Born: July 4, 1911, Petersburg, Alaska

Died: December 1, 1958, Juneau, Alaska

Elizabeth Peratrovich was a Tlingit Indian. When she was growing up, Native Alaskans faced **discrimination**. They could not live in some places. They could not work at some jobs. Only white people could. In 1945, Alaska's Senate was working on a new law. It would help stop discrimination. Some **senators** did not think the law was needed. Peratrovich made a speech. She told the senators how badly Native Alaskans were treated. She told them about a sign in a store. It said, "No dogs or Natives allowed." Her speech helped. The senators voted for the new law.

The Land

Alaska is separated from the rest of the United States by Canada. It is very far to the north. Fairbanks, Alaska, is almost as close to the North Pole as it is to Seattle, Washington.

Alaska is huge. It is more than twice the size of Texas, the next largest state. Alaska has long rivers, high mountains, and thick forests. It has a **panhandle** in the southeast. Alaska is a big and beautiful state.

Islands

This state has lots of islands. The Aleutian Islands reach out into the Pacific Ocean. They are farther west than any other part of the United

Mount McKinley is reflected in the waters of Wonder Lake in Denali National Park.

ALASKA

ARCTIC OCEAN

Point Barrow

Beaufort Sea

Chukchi Sea

Prudhoe Bay

Arctic National Wildlife Refugee

Brooks Range

RUSSIA

CANADA

Koyukuk R.

Yukon R.

Yukon R.

Nome

Yukon R.

Fairbanks

Tanana R.

Denali NP

Alaska Range

Mount McKinley

Wrangell Mountains

Yukon R.

Kuskokwim R.

Palmer

Anchorage

Valdez

Iliamna L.

Alaska Peninsula

Aleutian Range

The Range

Haines

Skagway

Juneau

Sitka

Petersburg

Gulf of Alaska

Bering Sea

Ketchikan

Aleutian Islands

PACIFIC OCEAN

N

W   E

S

SCALE/KEY

0   100 Miles

0   100 Kilometers

✪ State Capital

▲ Highest Point

▨ Mountains

States. One of the state's biggest cities is on an island. Only boats and airplanes can reach the city of Sitka.

Mountains

Alaska has many mountains. The Brooks Range crosses the state in the north. One southern range is the Alaska Range. Mount McKinley is in this range. At 20,320 feet (6,194 meters) high, it is North America's tallest peak.

The Central Region

Between Alaska's mountain ranges is the central region. This is a large, hilly area. It is full of river valleys and **muskeg**. Muskeg is a kind of swampy, soggy soil. The Yukon River runs through the central region. It is the longest river in the state.

The Coastal Plain

In the far northern part of Alaska is the Arctic coastal

Major Rivers

Yukon River
1,979 miles (3,184 km) long

Kusokwim River
600 miles (965 km) long

Tanana River
550 miles (885 km) long

plain. This region has many of Alaska's oil wells, but not many people. It is one of the coldest parts of Alaska. Much of the land is frozen all year long. Land like this is called **permafrost**. Point Barrow is in this area. It is farther north than any other part of the United States.

Earthquakes

Alaska has more earthquakes than the rest of the United States put together. In 1964, the state was rocked by a huge earthquake. It was the strongest ever to hit the United States. Anchorage and several other towns were very badly damaged.

Plants and Animals

Trees cover one-third of Alaska. The state tree is the Sitka spruce. It grows near the sea. In summer, Alaska's fields and plains are covered with wildflowers.

Alaska is a great place for animal watchers. Herds of caribou travel across the state each year. Moose, elk, beavers, wolves, and musk oxen live here. Alaska also is the home of some of the world's largest bears. It has Kodiak, grizzly, black, and polar bears.

More bald eagles live in Alaska than in all the other states. Salmon and trout swim in the rivers and lakes. Otters and seals play in the sea. Whales glide in the ocean.

FUN FACTS

Fire and Ice

When many people think of volcanoes, they think of Hawaii. In fact, Alaska has nearly 80 percent of all the active volcanoes in the United States. Alaska also has many glaciers. These are huge, slow-moving masses of ice. Two of the state's glaciers each cover more land than the whole state of Delaware!

This mother grizzly bear and her cubs are looking for fish along an Alaskan river. Grizzlies are beautiful, but they can be very dangerous.

Economy

Much of the money made in Alaska comes from the land. Oil, forests, and fish are the most important **natural resources** in the state. The people in Alaska want to protect these resources. They try to use them wisely.

Black Gold

Oil and natural gas are the most valuable resources in Alaska. They are important to the state's economy. Most of Alaska's oil comes from the far north. From there, the oil travels through a pipeline. It goes

This ship is in the port of Valdez. It's being loaded with oil from the Trans Alaska Pipeline System.

over 800 miles (1,287 km) to seaports in the south. The oil takes six days to go from one end of the pipeline to the other.

Forests, Fish, and Farms

Alaska's forests and fish are other important resources. Trees from forests are made into lumber and paper. Fish provide food. More fish are caught in Alaska than in any other state.

Alaska has some farms. In summer, the sun shines almost all day long. Often, the vegetables grow very large. Some carrots weigh 15 pounds (6.8 kilograms)!

Services

The biggest number of Alaskans have service jobs. People who teach, cook, and help tourists work in service jobs. Doctors and nurses are service workers, too.

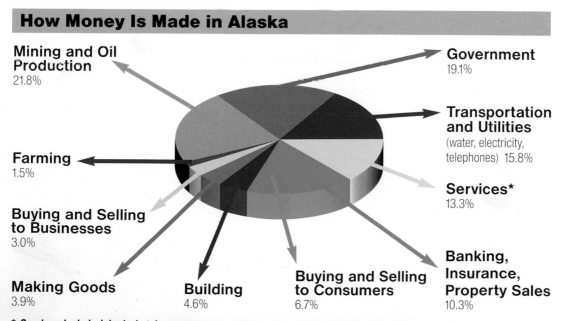

How Money Is Made in Alaska

Mining and Oil Production
21.8%

Government
19.1%

Transportation and Utilities
(water, electricity, telephones) 15.8%

Services*
13.3%

Farming
1.5%

Buying and Selling to Businesses
3.0%

Making Goods
3.9%

Building
4.6%

Buying and Selling to Consumers
6.7%

Banking, Insurance, Property Sales
10.3%

* Services include jobs in hotels, restaurants, auto repair, medicine, teaching, and entertainment.

Government

Alaska's state government is like the government of the United States. It has three parts, or branches.

Executive Branch

The executive branch carries out the laws of the state. It is led by the governor. The lieutenant governor helps the governor. Many other officials also work in this branch.

Legislative Branch

The legislative branch of the state government makes the laws. This

THE SEAL OF THE STATE OF ALASKA

A statue of a brown bear guards the State Capitol Building in Juneau.

These men and women hope to be elected to the Alaska State Senate. They are answering questions during a debate. Native Alaskan art covers the wall behind them.

branch has two parts. They are the Senate and the House of Representatives.

Judicial Branch

Courts and judges make up the judicial branch. They may decide whether a person who is accused of committing a crime is guilty. In Alaska, all courts are run by the state, rather than by towns or cities.

Local Governments

Alaskan cities have a mayor and a city council. Native corporations also are part of Alaska's local government. They help manage and protect the land, rights, and money of Native Alaskans.

ALASKA'S STATE GOVERNMENT

Executive		Legislative		Judicial	
Office	**Length of Term**	**Body**	**Length of Term**	**Court**	**Length of Term**
Governor	4 years	Senate (20 members)	4 years	Supreme (5 justices)	3, then 10 years
Lieutenant Governor	4 years	House of Representatives (40 members)	2 years	Court of Appeals (3 judges)	3, then 8 years

Things to See and Do

In a state with the biggest, the tallest, and the most, you'll never run out of things to see and do.

Museums and Parks

You can learn about Alaska's past at one of its great museums. The State Museum in Juneau tells about the history of this big state. It also has displays about Native Alaskan **culture**. At the Fairbanks Dog Mushing Museum, you can learn about sled dog racing. You can find out about the years of the Gold Rush at a historical park in Skagway.

A Native Alaskan carves a totem pole in Saxman Village, near Ketchikan.

Many hikers and climbers visit Denali National Park. In all, Alaska has fifteen national parks. They are great places to camp, hike, and enjoy the scenery.

Let's Celebrate!

Alaskans celebrate all year long. In fall, you can visit Haines for the Bald Eagle Festival. Check out the Ice Climbing Festival in Valdez in winter. In spring, go to the Festival of Native Arts in Fairbanks. You will see art and dancing by Native Alaskans. Alaska's State Fair takes place in Palmer every summer. You can enjoy games, rides, and animals.

Famous People of Alaska

Jewel

Born: Born: May 23, 1974, Payson, Utah

Jewel Kilcher moved to Alaska when she was very young. By age six, she was singing on stage with her parents. She became well known in 1989. She sang "Over the Rainbow" on a popular radio show. Her first album, *Pieces of You*, was released in 1995. Since then, Jewel has sung all over the country. She also has written two books.

Hikers on snowshoes watch the Northern Lights flash above the mountains.

Sports

Alaskans play all kinds of sports. The Eskimo-Indian Olympics take place in Fairbanks each year. These are tests of Native Alaskan skills. Each summer, at the Midnight Sun Baseball Classic in Fairbanks, games are played at night, without any lights! In November, college basketball comes to Anchorage. Some of the top teams compete in the Great Alaska Shootout.

Famous People of Alaska

Jack London

Born: January 12, 1876, San Francisco, California

Died: November 22, 1916, Santa Rosa, California

Jack London came to Alaska and the Yukon in 1897. He was looking for gold, but he found ideas for stories. He wrote about many of the people and things he saw in the far north. His writing made him famous. One of London's best-known books is *The Call of the Wild*. It is about a big dog named Buck. Another book he wrote, *White Fang*, is about a wolf. Both stories have been made into movies.

Melissa Rima from the city of North Pole gets past Hillarie Putnam from Wasilla and goes for the basket. The girls are competing in a high school playoff game in Anchorage.

Jeff King guides his team in the 2006 Iditarod Trail Sled Dog Race. This famous race is more than 1,000 miles (1,609 km) long. King and his dogs have won the Iditarod three times.

Snowmobiling, skiing, snowshoeing, and other winter sports are popular. The official state sport is sled dog racing. These races take place all winter long. The Iditarod Trail Sled Dog Race is the most famous. It takes from eight to fourteen days to finish this long race.

FUN FACTS

Racing Against Time

In January 1925, people in Nome were sick and dying. The medicine they needed was in Anchorage. That was almost 700 miles (1,127 km) away. All of the roads were closed. Airplanes could not be used. In Anchorage, a man put the medicine on his dogsled. He started for Nome as fast as he could go. He passed the medicine to another dog team. In all, twenty brave men and their dogs ran for six days in cold, snow, and darkness. The medicine got to Nome in time to help the people. Today, the Iditarod Trail Sled Dog Race remembers those men.

29

GLOSSARY

campus — the buildings and land that belong to a school

cannery — a factory where food is put into cans

caribou — a kind of very large deer

corporations — large businesses

culture — the language, beliefs, and actions of a people

discrimination — treating people badly because of their race or religion

kayaks — small boats, usually for just one person

minerals — valuable materials found on or under the ground, such as gold or oil

muskeg — soft, wet soil found in parts of Alaska

natural resources — valuable things found in nature that can be used by people, such as trees, fish, or oil

panhandle — a narrow area of land that juts out from the rest of the state

permafrost — ground that is frozen all year long

population — the number of people who live in a place, such as a state

rural — far away from big cities and large towns

senators — people elected to make laws

territory — an area of land that belongs to a country

Books

Alaska. Hello U.S.A. (series). Joyce Johnston (Lerner)

Alaska. Land of Liberty (series). Xavier W. Niz (Capstone Press)

Balto and the Great Race. Elizabeth Cody Kimmel (Random House Children's Books)

L Is for Last Frontier: An Alaska Alphabet. Discover America State by State (series). Carol Crane (Sleeping Bear Press)

Tlingit Indians. Native Americans (series). Suzanne Morgan Williams (Heinemann)

Web Sites

The Alaska Zoo Virtual Tour
www.alaskazoo.org/tour.htm

Enchanted Learning: Alaska
www.enchantedlearning.com/usa/states/alaska/

The Magnificent Moose Project
www.northstar.k12.ak.us/schools/awe/moose/moosepage.html

State of Alaska Kids Page
www.state.ak.us/local/kids/home.html

African Americans 14
airplanes 4, 16, 20, 29
Alaska Native Claims
    Settlement Act 12
Alaskan-Canadian
    Highway 10
Alaskan Native
    Brotherhood and
    Sisterhood 12
Alaska Range 20
Aleutian Islands 18, 20
Aleut people 6, 9, 14
Anchorage 15–17, 20–21,
    28, 29
Asian Americans 14

bears 21, 24
Benson, John "Benny" 9
Bering, Vitus 7, 13
Brooks Range 20
Butcher, Susan 11

Canada 8, 10, 15, 18
Congress, U.S. 9, 12

Denali National Park
    18, 27

eagles 21, 27
earthquakes 20–21
education 17
Exxon Valdez 11, 12

Fairbanks 18, 27, 28
fishing 8, 23
flag design 9
fur trading 7

gold 8–9, 26
Great Alaska Shootout 28
Gulf of Alaska 16

Haida people 6
Hispanics 14

Ice Climbing Festival 27
Iditarod Trail Sled Dog
    Race 11, 29
Inuit (Eskimos) 6, 14, 28

Japan 9–10
Jewel (Jewel Kilcher) 27
Juneau 5, 8, 9, 16, 17,
    24, 26
Juneau, Joe 8

kayaks 6
Ketchikan 26
King, Jeff 29

London, Jack 28

"midnight sun" 18, 23
Mount McKinley
    4, 18, 20
museums 26

Native Alaskans 6–7, 12,
    14, 17, 25–28
Nome 29
Northern Lights 27
North Pole (town) 28

oil (petroleum) 10–12,
    15, 20, 22–23

Pacific Ocean 18
Peratrovich, Elizabeth 17
Petersburg 17
potlatches 7
Prudhoe Bay 10

religion 16–17
Russia 7–8, 10, 15

Saxman Village 26
Sitka 7, 20
Skagway 8, 26
sled dog racing 10, 29
Smith, Soapy 8
sports 28–29

Tlingit people 6, 17
Trans Alaska Pipeline
    System 22–23

Valdez 22, 27
volcanoes 21

World War II 9–10

Yukon River 20